* WE ARE AMERICA *

Mexican Americans

TRISTAN BOYER BINNS

Heinemann Library
Chicago, Illinois

Customer Service 888-454-2279

Visit our website at www.heinemannlibrary.com

Created by the publishing team at Heinemann Library
Designed by Roslyn Broder
Photo research by Scott Braut
Printed and Bound in the United States by Lake Book Manufacturing, Inc.

07 06 05 04 03
10 9 8 7 6 5 4 3 2 1

Library of Congress Cataloging-in-Publication Data
Boyer Binns, Tristan, 1968-
Mexican Americans / Tristan Boyer Binns.
p. cm. -- (We are America)
Summary: An overview of the history and daily lives of Mexican people who immigrated to the United States.
Includes bibliographical references (p.) and index.
ISBN 1-40340-163-2 (lib. bdg.) -- ISBN 1-40340-418-6 (pbk.)
1. Mexican Americans--History--Juvenile literature. 2. Mexican Americans--Social life and customs--Juvenile literature. [1. Mexican Americans.] I. Title. II. Series.
E184.M5 B69 2002
973'.046872--dc21
2002004142

Acknowledgments
The author and publishers are grateful to the following for permission to reproduce copyright material: pp. 4, 5 Courtesy of Bertha Baillie and María Hinojosa; p. 6 Corbis; p. 8 Courtesy of the Museum of New Mexico, negative number 22468; p. 10 Library of Congress; p. 11 Aultman Collection/El Paso Public Library/AP/WideWorld Photos; p. 12 Bettmann/Corbis; p. 14 Russell Lee/Corbis; p. 15 AP/WideWorld Photos; p. 16 Shel Hershorn/UT Austin/Archive Photos/Hulton Archive; p. 17 Dennis Poroy/AP/WideWorld Photos; p. 18 Spencer Grant/PhotoEdit, Inc.; p. 19 Alan Greth/AP/WideWorld Photos; p. 20 Sandy Felsenthal/Corbis; p. 21 Lawrence Migdale/Stone/Getty Images; p. 22 Catherine Karnow/Corbis; p. 23 Zephyr Picture/Index Stock Imagery, Inc.; p. 24 H. Scott Hoffmann/News & Record/AP/WideWorld Photos; p. 25 A. Ramey/PhotoEdit, Inc.; p. 26 David Young-Wolff/PhotoEdit, Inc.; p. 27 Lawrence Migdale/Stone/Getty Images; p. 28 Ted Thai/TimePix; p. 29 Courtesy of CNN

Cover photographs provided by Robert Lifson/Heinemann Library (bck) and Ariel Skelley/Corbis

Special thanks to Barry Moreno of the Ellis Island Immigration Museum for his comments in preparation of this book and Bertha Baillie. Tristan Boyer Binns thanks Stephanie Pasternak, Ruben Gutierrez, Esther Medina, and María Hinojosa.

Some quotations and material used in this book come from the following sources. In some cases, quotes have been abridged for clarity: p. 10 *Memories for Tomorrow* by Margaret Beeson, Marjorie Adams, and Rosalie King (Detroit, Mich.: Blaine Ethridge Books, 1983); p. 15 *Between Two Cultures* by John J. Poggie Jr. (Tucson, Ariz.: University of Arizona Press, 1973); p. 17, 25 *Mexican Voices/American Dreams* by Marilyn P. Davis (New York: Henry Holt & Company, 1990).

Some words are shown in bold, **like this.** You can find out what they mean by looking in the glossary.

On the cover of this book, a Mexican-American family is shown in 1996. A recent photo taken in the Pilsen neighborhood, which is home to Chicago's largest Mexican-American population, is featured in the background.

Contents

María's Move

María Hinojosa's father, Raul, was an ear doctor. The hospital that he worked at in Mexico City closed. He didn't want to move his family, but he couldn't find a job in Mexico. He took a job in Chicago, Illinois, in 1965. María's mother, with Maria and her brothers and sisters, took a plane to join him. Maria was one year old.

Maria, right, is about three years old in this picture of her and her sister, Bertha Elena, taken in Boston.

I could see my friends who were also different in school and know I was like them. Chinese, Japanese, Jewish, Mexican—our differences made us special.

— María Hinojosa

> Having Campbell's soup or Chef Boyardee spaghetti was a special treat. I wanted to eat them because that's what my friends were eating. It made me feel like everyone else.
>
> —María Hinojosa

Unlike many Mexican **immigrants,** María's family had enough money to live in a nice neighborhood. They also visited Chicago's Mexican barrio, or neighborhood, every week to shop for food. Every year, the family went back to Mexico to visit friends and family. Like many of the five million Mexicans who have immigrated to the United States since 1960, María grew up feeling comfortable in both countries.

The Hinojosa family posed for this picture in 1969. Bertha had just graduated from eighth grade. María is in the center of the picture in a white dress.

The First Mexican Americans

The place we know as Mexico was first **settled** by Indians. People from Spain sailed from Europe in the early 1500s and took control of the area. Many Spanish people married the native Indians. Their children became the people we now know as Mexicans. The Spanish moved into areas we know today as California, Texas, and New Mexico. The weather and land there was like Mexico and Spain. The new settlers knew how to farm and make homes in these places.

*In the 1770s, people traveling from Mexico built the **Mission** San Juan Capistrano in California as a center for business, farming, education, and religion.*

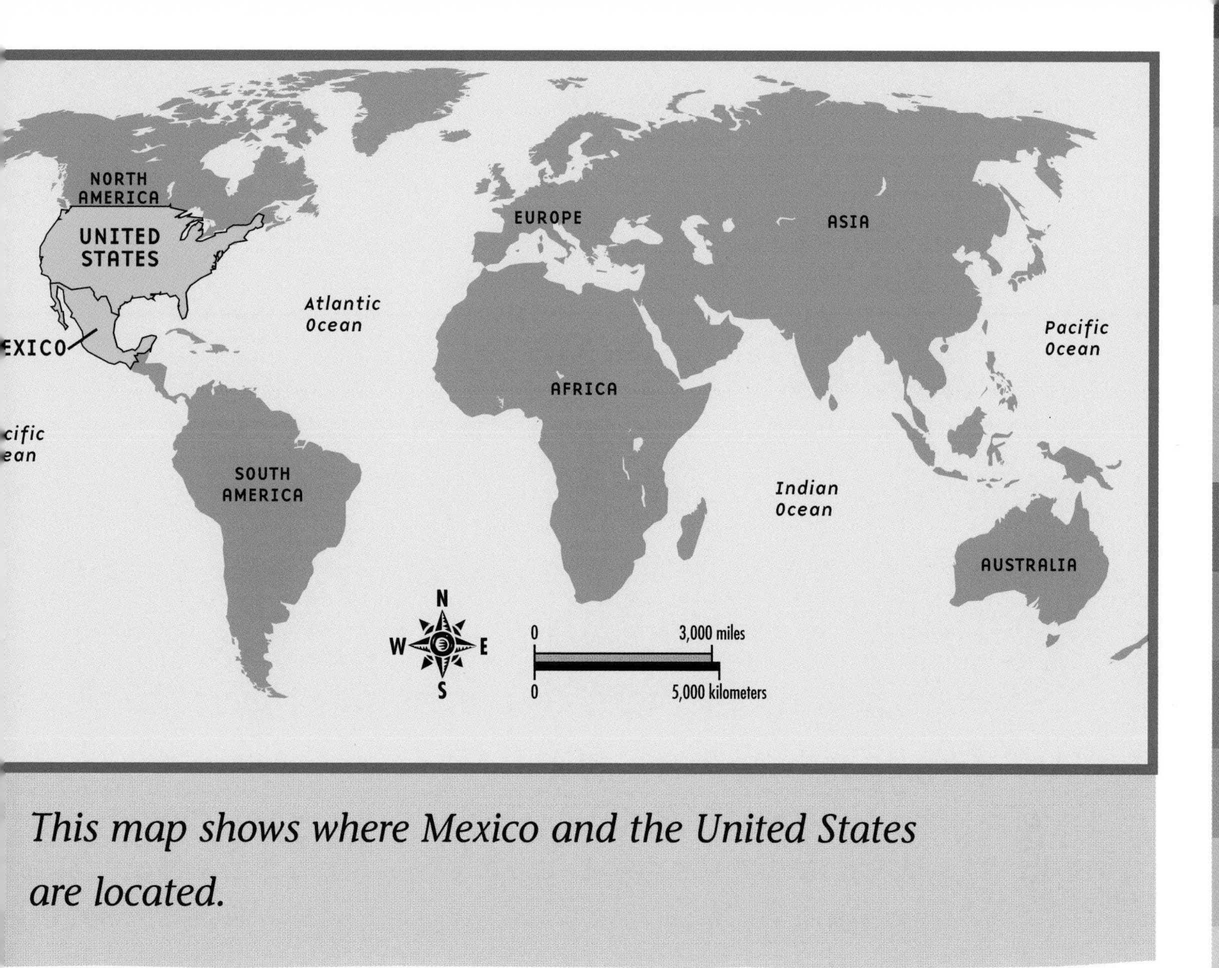

This map shows where Mexico and the United States are located.

In the early 1800s, the people of Mexico wanted to form their own country and not be controlled by Spain. In 1821, Mexico became an **independent** country. Soon after, the United States went to war with Mexico and won. Mexico gave the United States about half of its land in 1848. Suddenly, all the Mexicans living there became United States citizens. A citizen is a person who is a member of a country and who can vote in that country's elections.

Losing Land

At first, some of the new Mexican Americans helped run the local government. They got to keep their land. But soon, there were more white American **settlers** than Mexican Americans. The United States made Mexican Americans prove that they owned their land. Many of them could not do this, so they lost their land. Others lost land because settlers started living on their land and would not leave.

Few children in farming families went to school because they had to help with work. In the late 1800s, this family lived in an area that is now in the state of New Mexico.

Time Line

1519–1821 Spain rules Mexico. Mexican land stretches from California to Texas and as far north as Utah.

1848 Mexico loses a war with the United States and gives about half its land to the U.S. Mexicans living in these lands become U.S. citizens.

1910–1920 Mexican **revolution** forces many Mexicans to move to the U.S.

1910–1930 About 700,000 Mexicans **immigrate** to the U.S.

1965 First limits put on number of immigrants allowed from Mexico. Since 1960, over 4.5 million Mexicans have immigrated to the U.S.

2000 About 170,000 Mexicans immigrate to the U.S.

By 1900, most government leaders were white Americans. Mexican Americans also couldn't vote in some places. As a result, they had no say in how things were run. There were fights between Mexican Americans and white Americans over how land should be used. Many Mexican-American cowboys worked for white Americans who raised cattle.

In 1848, about 15,000 Mexican Americans lived in California. By 1852, more than 260,000 people lived there. People from all over the world came looking for gold during the **Gold Rush.** The people who came often ruined the farmland of Mexican Americans.

More Immigrants

In Mexico, very few people owned land. Most people made very little money. Bosses were often unfair and people had no way to object. By the early 1900s, many Mexicans went to the United States to find work. They helped lay railroad tracks and worked on farms and in mines.

On the hill where the animals wandered loose, w
rode them like cowboys dc
. . . now and then they thr
us off. We spent the time very happily and had a lo
of fun when we weren't working.

—Sabino Martinez Array
talking about his childho
in Mexico in the early 190

This Mexican man used a cart and a donkey in 1912 to move from a city in Mexico to the United States.

People in Mexico left their homes because of the revolution and came to the United States. These Mexican people are walking along railroad tracks near El Paso, Texas, in about 1912.

In 1910, a **revolution** broke out against the Mexican government. Many people wanted the land in Mexico to be shared by everyone. The revolution grew into a war. More than one million Mexicans died. Crops and land were ruined and people were hungry. Because of the war, it was not safe to stay in Mexico. Many Mexicans went north to the United States as **refugees.** More than 700,000 Mexicans **immigrated** to the United States between 1910 and 1930.

Life in the United States

Most of the Mexican **immigrants** worked in farming. They also helped build the **canals** used to bring water to crops in the southwest United States. Many grew and picked cotton in Texas and fruits and vegetables in the West. Because they were Mexican, they were paid less than what white Americans would get for the same amount of work. Even so, they still earned more than they would have in Mexico.

These Mexican farmworkers are picking cotton in Texas in 1919.

Mexican Immigration to the United States

This map shows some of the areas in the United States that Mexicans first moved to and where many still live today.

Most Mexican Americans in the United States lived in places with similar weather and land to their homes in Mexico. But in the 1920s, many immigrants from Mexico went north to Illinois, Michigan, Indiana, and Ohio. They worked making cars, tires, and steel. By 1929, more than 20,000 Mexican Americans lived in Chicago.

The United States **Border Patrol** was formed in 1924 with 450 members. The patrol's job was to stop **illegal immigrants** from crossing the 2,000-mile (3,225-kilometer) border between Mexico and the United States. Today, the patrol has about 9,500 men and women.

Farmworkers

In 1929, many companies in the United States went out of business. Many U.S. citizens did not have jobs. The citizens wanted anyone who was not a citizen to leave, so they could have any jobs there were in the U.S. Hundreds of thousands of Mexican farmworkers were sent back to Mexico. A lot of them were **illegal immigrants** from Mexico who farm owners in the United States didn't have to pay much.

The boy in this picture was picking carrots in 1939 on a farm in Texas.

Bracero *workers like these young men picking beets in California had to get a doctor's checkup before they could begin work. The* bracero *program ran from 1941 to 1964.*

During **World War Two,** more than 300,000 Mexican Americans fought for the United States. Thousands of other men fought, too. There were not enough farmworkers, so the Mexican and U.S. governments started the *bracero* program. *Bracero* means "strong arm," or worker. Mexicans got passes to work in the United States for 60 or 90 days.

We used to pick red grapes and black grapes and put them on trays. Then the sun would dry them and make raisins . . . We got paid one cent a tray.

—Ramón Gonzales, talking about his work in California in 1931, when he was ten years old

Legal or Illegal?

In 1965, the United States government decided to limit how many people could **immigrate** from Mexico each year. But thousands of Mexican people still wanted to go to the United States. They could make up to four times as much money as they could in Mexico. Mexicans still immigrated legally, or lawfully, but many more couldn't get permission to go. They immigrated illegally, or unlawfully, so they could earn more money in the United States.

Some Mexican people, like this woman shown in 1967, come into the United States every day to work but still live in homes in Mexico.

This picture shows cars in 1997 lined up waiting to enter California from the city of Tijuana, Mexico.

Today, legal immigrants come in cars and on airplanes. Many **illegal immigrants** try to walk or swim across Mexico's **border.** The **Border Patrol** catches many illegal immigrants and sends them back to Mexico. In 1986, the United States government passed a law that said all illegal immigrants who came to the country before 1982 could stay in the United States. By 1990, about 13 million Americans had Mexican **ancestors.**

But coming to the United States—I'll never forget that. I was really afraid. These people were speaking this other language, they dressed differently, acted differently. It's like going to another planet, you know.

—Cesar Rosas, the lead singer for a band called Los Lobos, who immigrated with his family in 1962

The Way of Life

Mexican Americans live in every state in the United States. Many Mexicans live in big cities such as Chicago and New York. Others live in smaller towns and work on farms or in factories. Some own businesses or work in government jobs. The people in government try to make life better for other Mexican Americans by passing laws that protect them.

Loretta Sanchez, a government leader from California, is shown shaking hands with people at a Mexican ***Independence*** *Day parade.*

César Chávez was a Mexican-American farmworker. He was one of the first Mexican Americans to help farmworkers get better pay and safer jobs.

Many Mexicans live in Mexico and cross the **border** every day to go to work or school in a town in the United States. Others travel north in the United States each year to pick fruit and vegetables. Many Mexican Americans have jobs and homes in the United States and go back to Mexico to see family members.

Homes and Families

Many Mexican **immigrants** move into neighborhoods where other Mexican Americans live. Sometimes these are small towns in the country. Other times they are parts of a big city. In a city, Mexican neighborhoods are often called barrios.

There were all these kids from Mexico in Chilton who were f the very same neighborhood i [Mexico], so I was with kids fr my neighborhood. People cam there by word-of-mouth—that' why there were so many peopl we knew there.

—Ruben Gutierrez, who mo to the small town of Chil Texas, with his family in 1 when he was nine years

This boy in the center is waving a Mexican flag during a Mexican ***Independence*** *Day parade in Chicago in 1995.*

This Mexican-American family is making masks that are used in a traditional Mexican celebration called the Day of the Dead.

New immigrants sometimes live with friends or family before they move into their own homes. Most Mexican Americans think their families are very important. Children usually grow up feeling very close to their parents, grandparents, **godparents,** and aunts and uncles. They sometimes visit family members in Mexico and learn about the history and **traditions** of Mexico.

Working and Playing

Mexican Americans work at all kinds of jobs. They work as teachers, doctors, and lawyers, just to name a few. Others work in farming, helping to grow and pick the food that people eat. Sometimes, whole families travel and work on farms together during the picking season. Other families own small businesses, like grocery stores or house-cleaning businesses. Mexican Americans also help to build houses and other buildings.

This Mexican American owns a grocery store in Los Angeles, California.

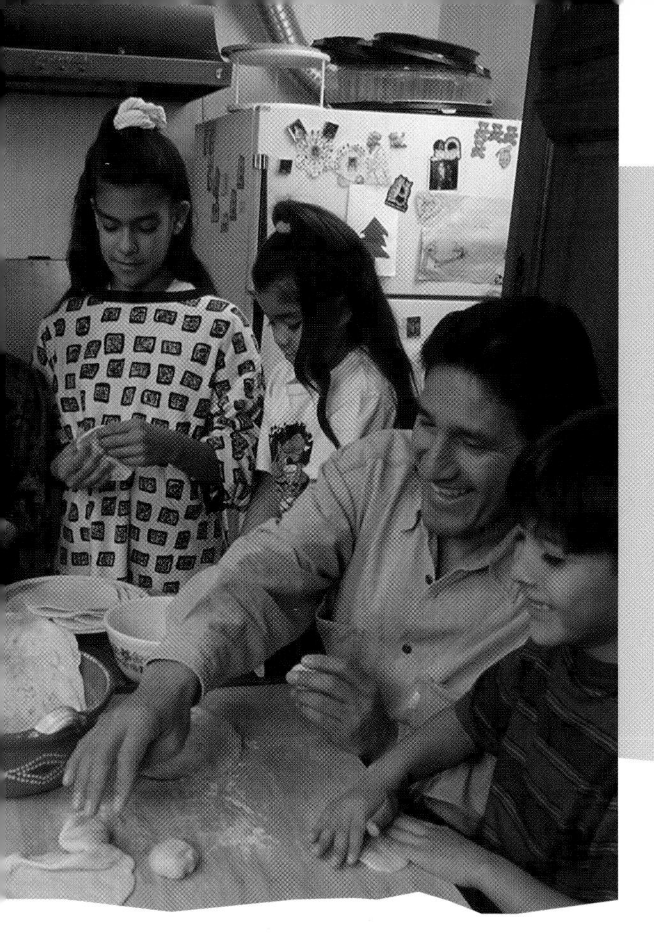

This Mexican-American family is making tortillas, which are round, flat pieces of bread made from corn or wheat flour. They are rolled up with a filling and eaten hot.

Like most children, Mexican-American kids like to play with their friends after school. Evenings may be spent doing homework, watching TV, and spending time with family members. Many families eat dinner together every night. Food at home is often a mix of **traditional** Mexican foods and American foods.

As soon as I came here I remember eating a hot dog and I had no idea what that was. At first I was like, "What is this?" The other thing was hamburgers. I'd never seen hamburgers like in the states. They were just great. The best thing was Dairy Queen, which are big hamburger joints in Texas. Eating pizza—it was great.

—Ruben Gutierrez

Going to School

Like many **immigrants,** Mexican children often cannot speak English when they first come to the United States. School can be hard if the children do not know English. Spanish-speaking friends help them learn how things work at school in the United States. Many children take special classes in which they only study English. Adults can also take classes to learn English.

Many students in the United States, like this girl in North Carolina, study Spanish, the language spoken in Mexico.

This Mexican-American boy is learning how to use a computer at his school in California.

I went to sixth grade in Mexico and now I'm in seventh here. I didn't know any English, but I found some friends who told me which rooms I had to go to. There are other kids here from Mexico, so I don't feel lonely and it's easy to make friends. All of my teachers are very nice too. It's a little bit different here. In Mexico girls don't run or play basketball or volleyball, only the boys.

—Madelin, who moved to Oceanside, California, in the 1980s

In Texas I struggled a lot in English and all the other courses. After eight months, I was feeling more confident. I continued to ask a lot of questions like my parents always told me to do. I remember having a dictionary with me all the time. When I didn't have it with me I would ask teachers, "What does that mean?"

—Ruben Gutierrez

Celebrations

Many Mexican Americans in the United States celebrate the same holidays that people in Mexico do. *Cinco de Mayo,* May 5, is a celebration of a battle that the Mexican people won in 1862. Mexican **Independence** Day on September 16 celebrates Mexico's freedom from Spain. *Dia de Los Muertos,* the Day of the Dead, is celebrated on November 1 and 2. People make their favorite foods. They think about and remember family members and relatives who have died.

These kids are dancing in ***traditional*** *Mexican clothing at a* Cinco de Mayo *festival in Los Angeles.*

This girl is lighting candles as part of the Day of the Dead.

When many Mexican-American girls turn fifteen, they have a special birthday party called a *quinceañera.* There is a church service and a lot of dancing. The girl talks about people who are important to her. Mexican Americans celebrate Christmas like many other Americans do. Some also eat special foods, like *buñuelos,* a kind of doughnut, or *tamales,* meat and dough wrapped in cornhusks.

One of the biggest holidays in Mexico is Christmas. In Mexico you start by celebrating Posada beginning December 7 with the community of the town . . . You go to someone's house and they feed you cookies and hot chocolate. Each night you'd go to a different house and this would go on and on till the 23rd. And on the 24th you'd do it yourself with your family at your own house.

—Ruben Gutierrez

María's Story

María also loves spending time at home with her two children.

Because she came from Mexico and had a different way of life than many Americans, María Hinojosa felt that she was different from most Americans. Stories about people like her were never told on television or in the newspapers. María decided to become a **reporter** to tell the stories of people who came from different countries and who lived different lives. Now, she works as a television reporter and a radio-show host.

Like many Mexican Americans, María thinks talking to family members who live far away and visiting them is important. María wants her children to feel the same way. She also helps them understand that the Mexicans who live around them in New York City are all their *paisanos,* which means "friends from the same country."

I grew up feeling invisible. I always wanted to be a reporter so I could tell stories I wanted to see and hear. I want young kids who feel invisible to see themselves in my work.

—María Hinojosa

My kids say good night to their cousins, aunts, uncles, and grandparents every night even though they live far away.

—María Hinojosa

Maria works as a reporter for CNN and National Public Radio, two news stations.

Mexican Immigration Chart

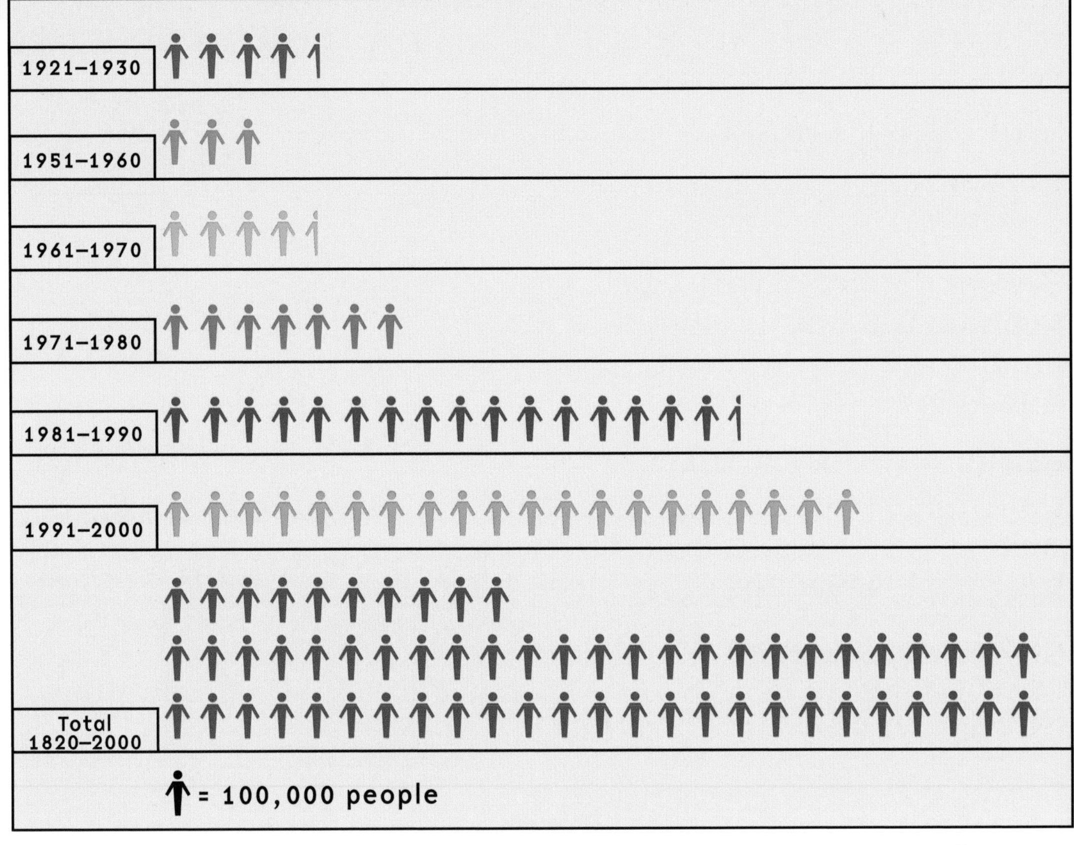

The biggest number of Mexican ***immigrants*** *came to the United States in the 1990s.*

Source: U.S. Immigration and Naturalization Service

More Books to Read

Atkin, S. Beth. *Voices from the Fields: Children of Migrant Farmworkers Tell Their Stories.* New York: Little, Brown & Company, 2000.

Hoyt-Goldsmith, Diane. *Las Posadas: A Mexican-American Christmas Celebration.* New York: Holiday House, 1999.

McCulloch, Julie. *A World of Recipes: Mexico.* Chicago: Heinemann Library, 2001.

Unger, J. *I Am Mexican American.* New York: Rosen Publishing Group, 1997.

Glossary

ancestor person who you are related to and who was born before you, like your mother, father, or grandparent

border place where two countries or states meet

Border Patrol group formed to prevent illegal, or unlawful, immigrants from getting into the United States

canal ditch dug and filled with water so that boats can cross a stretch of land. Canals are also used to get water to crops.

godparent man or woman who promises to make sure a child gets a religious education

Gold Rush time from 1848 to 1859 when gold was found in California. People from all over the world went there to try to get rich.

illegal immigrant person who is not allowed to live in a foreign country but who tries to anyway

immigrate to come to a country to live there for a long time. A person who immigrates is an immigrant.

independent condition of being free from the rule of other countries, governments, or people. The state of being independent is called independence.

mission place where religious leaders live and work to spread a new religion to the people of a country or area

refugee person who has to go away from his or her country and who can't return home because he or she could be hurt

reporter person who tells news stories in newspapers or on radio or television

revolution fight to change the ways a country's rulers act

settler person who moves into, or settles, a new part of a country and who is among the first to live there

tradition belief or practice handed down through the years from one generation to the next

World War Two war fought from 1939 to 1945 by Germany, Japan, and Italy on one side and the United States, Great Britain, China, and the Soviet Union on the other

Index